The Weird Wild West: Tall Tales and Legends about the Frontier

By Sean McLachlan and Charles River Editors

1880s picture of a cowboy in the American West

About Charles River Editors

Charles River Editors provides superior editing and original writing services across the digital publishing industry, with the expertise to create digital content for publishers across a vast range of subject matter. In addition to providing original digital content for third party publishers, we also republish civilization's greatest literary works, bringing them to new generations of readers via ebooks.

Sign up here to receive updates about free books as we publish them, and visit Our Kindle Author Page to browse today's free promotions and our most recently published Kindle titles.

About the Author

Sean McLachlan has spent much of his life in Arizona and Missouri, working as an archaeologist and tracing legends of the Old West. Now a full-time writer, he's the author of many history books and novels, including *A Fine Likeness*, a Civil War novel with a touch of the weird. He did not qualify for a Jackalope hunting license, so don't ask, but for more information, check out his Amazon page and blog.

Introduction

A picture of 19th century homesteaders

The Weird Wild West

Space may be the final frontier, but no frontier has ever captured the American imagination like the "Wild West", which still evokes images of dusty cowboys, outlaws, gunfights, gamblers, and barroom brawls over 100 years after the West was settled. A constant fixture in American pop culture, the 19th century American West continues to be vividly and colorful portrayed not just as a place but as a state of mind.

Even for those who travel through the West today, there are plenty of traces of the old times. Ghost towns still stand in remote parts of the desert and prairie, Native American rock art still tell their mute legends, and old prospectors' mines still dot the hillsides. Even some of the places' names, such as Bloody Basin, Arizona and Soldier's Hill, New Mexico, have their stories to tell. In November 2014, one lucky archaeologist at Nevada's Great Basin National Park spotted an old rifle leaning against a pine tree; the sun and wind had weathered the wooden stock until it was as gray as the tree trunk, making it almost invisible to passersby. When the gun was examined, it turned out to be a Winchester rifle. The serial number was still legible and records showed that it had been manufactured and shipped in 1882. Some prospector or hunter had set the rifle against a tree more than a century ago and never came back for it. It had been leaning there ever since.

As popular as works about the West remain today, the Wild West captured the imagination of people all the way back to the days when it really was wild. Even in the 19th century, its fame spread thanks to dime novels, travelogues, Wild West shows, and theater plays, and people were thrilled by tales of exploration and gunfights. Naturally, in the process of settling the frontier, the adventures contained countless numbers of strange stories, ranging from tales of monsters and lost mines to those about hidden cities and men coming back from the dead. It was a vast, unexplored country, and many mysteries could hide in the unmapped mountain ranges and seemingly endless plains.

The Weird Wild West: Tall Tales and Legends about the Frontier is a collection of tales about America's frontier that range from the possible to the downright ridiculous. Some are adaptations of old folk tales immigrants brought with them or creations of overly eager newspaper reporters, but many have their basis in fact. Along with pictures and a bibliography, you will learn about the Weird Wild West like never before, in no time at all.

The Weird Wild West: Tall Tales and Legends about the Frontier
About Charles River Editors
About the Author
Introduction
    Chapter 1: Lost Mines and Buried Treasure
    Chapter 2: Bumbling Bandits and Freaky Fellers
    Chapter 3: Jesse James is Alive
    Chapter 4: So is Everyone Else
    Chapter 5: Lost Civilizations
    Chapter 6: The Thunderbird
    Chapter 7: Other Strange Creatures
    Bibliography

Chapter 1: Lost Mines and Buried Treasure

In the 19th century, hundreds of thousands of people moved west looking to make a fortune, and of course, some of them found it. There were silver rushes, and in Missouri there was even a lead rush, but perhaps not surprisingly, the Great Missouri Lead Rush never got made into a movie. Of course, One of the most important and memorable events of the United States' westward push across the frontier came with the discovery of gold in the lands that became California in January 1848. Located thousands of miles away from the country's power centers on the east coast at the time, the announcement came a month before the Mexican-American War had ended, and among the very few Americans that were near the region at the time, many of them were Army soldiers who were participating in the war and garrisoned there. San Francisco was still best known for being a Spanish military and missionary outpost during the colonial era, and only a few hundred called it home. Mexico's independence, and its possession of those lands, had come only a generation earlier.

Everything changed almost literally overnight. While the Mexican-American War technically concluded with a treaty in February 1848, the announcement brought an influx of an estimated 90,000 "Forty-Niners" to the region in 1849, hailing from other parts of America and even as far away as Asia. All told, an estimated 300,000 people would come to California over the next few years, as men dangerously trekked thousands of miles in hopes of making a fortune, and in a span of months, San Francisco's population exploded, making it one of the first mining boomtowns to truly spring up in the West. This was a pattern that would repeat itself across the West anytime a mineral discovery was made, from the Southwest and Tombstone to the Dakotas and Deadwood. Of course, that was made possible by the collective memory of the original California gold rush.

Despite the mythology and the romantic portrayals that helped make the California Gold Rush, most of the individuals who came to make a fortune struck out instead. The gold rush was a boon to business interests, which ensured important infrastructure developments like the railroad and the construction of westward paths, but ultimately, it also meant that big business reaped most of the profits associated with mining the gold. While the Forty-Niners are often remembered for panning gold out of mountain streams, it required advanced mining technology for most to make a fortune.

Nevertheless, the California Gold Rush became an emblem of the American Dream, and the notion that Americans could obtain untold fortunes regardless of their previous social status. As historian H.W. Brands said of the impact the gold rush had on Americans at the time, "The old American Dream ... was the dream of the Puritans, of Benjamin Franklin's 'Poor Richard'... of men and women content to accumulate their modest fortunes a little at a time, year by year by year. The new dream was the dream of instant wealth, won in a twinkling by audacity and good luck... [it] became a prominent part of the American psyche only after Sutter's Mill." While the gold rush may not have made every Forty-Niner rich, the events still continue to influence the country's collective mentality.

Illustration in Harpers Ferry of a "49er" panning gold

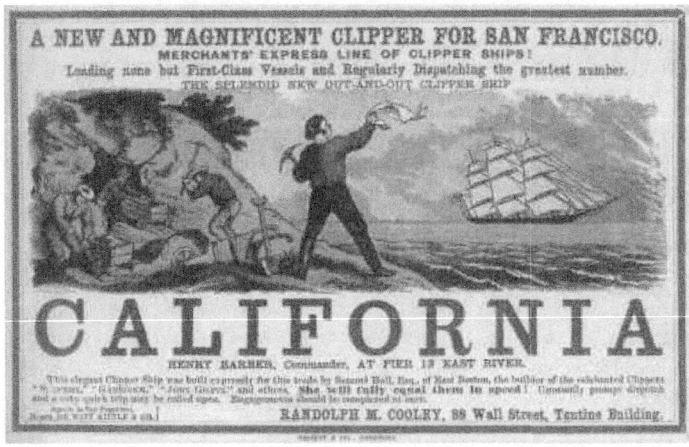

Advertisement for sailing to San Francisco amidst the Gold Rush

A man panning for gold

For the most part, prospectors had a hard life with very little financial reward, so they were prone to exaggerate the luck of those who did strike the Mother Lode and stir up rumors of vast riches just waiting to be picked up. If all the stories were to be believed, the West is honeycombed with lost mines, hidden caches of Confederate gold, Indian treasure, and broad veins of gold and silver.

While it probably wouldn't behoove anyone to devote time and resources to a search, there certainly is some buried treasure out there. The Old West had plenty of outlaws who needed to hide their loot, after all, and a prime example could be found in Genoa, Nevada. This mining town attracted more than its fair share of robbers in the late 19th century thanks to the prosperous gold mines in the forested hills next to the town. Every week the gold ore was shipped out, and from the other direction came a wagon or stagecoach carrying the paymaster's money, usually in gold coins. The pay wagon kept getting robbed, so the paymaster decided to get sneaky by hiding the entire payroll, some $20,000 in $20 gold coins, in a keg marked "nails" and putting it on a shipment of everyday supplies. Somehow a pair of robbers got wind of this trick and lay in wait for the supply wagon. They held it up, grabbed the keg, and headed for the hills outside of town.

A search of the hills found no trace of the robbers or their loot, and the matter was all but forgotten until many years later when a miner, lying on his deathbed in Montana, confessed to the crime. He related how he and another man hid in the hills, opened up the keg, and each took $1,000 out of it. They then buried the keg near a tall pine and fled the territory, promising to come back once the law had stopped looking for them. For reasons he didn't make clear, neither he nor his accomplice ever returned.

When this story made it back to Genoa, locals scoured the hillsides, digging near every pine tree they could find. None discovered any treasure, and in 1882 an avalanche knocked down many of the trees and moved large sections of the slopes. The treasure was probably moved with it, and no fewer than three times in the 20th century, gold coins were uncovered in different locations on those hills, so it seems the avalanche broke open the keg and scattered the coins. The biggest find came in 1961 when a lucky fellow happened upon $2,000 in $20 gold coins. It's safe to assume that more coins are still up there, scattered across the hillside, so anyone who likes to use a metal detector might want to start around Genoa.

Another tale of treasure with its basis in truth is that of the Yocum Dollar. Back in the early 19th century, the four Yocum brothers - Solomon, Jacob, Jess, and Mike - settled in the White River valley in the Ozarks, and they were among the first white men in the region. They were soon joined by the Delaware tribe, which the federal government relocated to the Ozarks from their homeland back east. To compensate the Delaware for forcing them off their native land, the government paid the tribe $4,000 in U.S. silver coins every year, with the chiefs getting some extra coins. The Yocum brothers smelled money and moved onto the Delaware reservation, where they set up a still and started selling bootleg whiskey, for which the Delaware paid with U.S. silver coins. Since selling alcohol to Native Americans was illegal, the Yocum brothers covered their tracks by melting the coins down and recasting them as Yocum Dollars.

Making one's own money wasn't illegal at the time, as there was a shortage of U.S. government dollars (in the Ozarks many people used Spanish coins coming up with merchants on the Santa Fe Trail), so local banks and even stores printed their own currency. Most of these were paper notes of dubious value. Businesses often shut down or got greedy and flooded the market with notes, but people much preferred the Yocum dollars, which were plentiful, made by a respected local family, and were a purer grade of silver than the U.S. dollars. Of course, the Yocum brothers didn't reveal that their silver was coming from illegal sales of alcohol on the reservation, so they made up a tale of a silver cave they supposedly bought from the Delaware for two horses, some blankets, and soap.

In hindsight, their story smacks of frontier racism, as the Delaware were already familiar enough with white culture to know the value of silver. At the time, however, many locals believed the story, and their eyes opened wide when the Yocum brothers told how one vein was 20 feet long and the other was 30 feet. Sometimes the Yocum brothers would go off into the countryside, telling everyone they were setting out to do some mining, and some of their greedy neighbors would follow them to learn the secret of the cave. Of course, the Yocum brothers would simply slip away into the rough hill and make a big circle back home, after which they could sit back and enjoy the sight of their neighbors straggling back a few days later, exhausted and penniless.

The local Indian agent wasn't fooled by all these shenanigans and kicked the Yocum brothers off the reservation, but all that achieved was to make the Delaware walk a bit further to get their whiskey. The family business continued until 1831, when the tribe moved to a new reservation in Kansas, but by then the Yocum family had become the richest family in the region.

While the Yocum brothers settled down to more legal pursuits such as farming and milling, the legend of their silver cave never died. Some say that on his deathbed, Solomon Yocum gave directions to the cave to his grandson William, who drew a map from Solomon's description. For some reason he never went looking for it, but in the early 20th century one of his descendants, Joseph Yocum, did take up the search. By then, development and ambitious dam projects had changed the landscape beyond recognition, so the map was of no use. Moreover, the map has since disappeared, and so have the Yocum dollars. A few were found by workmen in an old cabin in 1923, and one went on sale at a coin dealer in 1984, but since then, none have been seen. Most were probably melted down for their silver and now the coins, and the mine, have passed into legend.

While some of the Genoa gold has been found and the Yocum coins have probably all been recycled, in the Guadalupe Mountains in western Texas there's a mine that's still waiting to be rediscovered. Anyone who finds it will be rich, and it sure made Ben Sublett rich. Sublett arrived in Odessa, west Texas, in the 1870s. He was a widower with three children who made a meager living hunting game to supply the workers on the new Texas and Pacific Railroad, along with other odd jobs and a bit of prospecting on the side. The gold bug turned out to be more attractive, and he'd often leave his children with neighbors for weeks at a time while he tried his luck prospecting. Most of the time he'd return with only a bit of gold dust or a measly nugget or two, worth just enough to give him a night in the saloon. The next day he'd stock up on beans and coffee at the general store, give his children his last bit of money, and head back out to try his luck again.

His usual stomping grounds were the Guadalupe Mountains, 70 miles west of Odessa. These rough mountains run for a hundred miles and hide countless canyons and cul-de-sacs. Water is scarce. Even today parts of the range are rarely visited, and back in Sublett's day it was all but unexplored. The most visible mountain is Guadalupe Peak, the highest point in Texas, rising 9,500 feet above sea level just south of the border with New Mexico.

Guadalupe Peak

The Guadalupe Mountains

One time in 1881, he came back from a prospecting trip with his head high instead of bowed, and with a smile on his face instead of a frown. He went as usual straight for his favorite saloon—Sublett was considered a hard drinker even by the standards of those hard-drinking days—and announced that it was his round. In fact, he didn't just buy drinks for his friends, he bought them for the whole town, as much as everyone could drink. When the bartender asked how he was going to pay for all this hooch, Sublett grinned. He pulled out a buckskin pouch and clunked it on the bar. It was full nuggets of the purest gold. Now it was the bartender's turn to grin.

When asked where he'd struck the Mother Lode, all he would say is that it had been in the Guadalupe Mountains. From then on, Sublett never worked, but every few months he'd ride out towards the mountains and return a few days or weeks later with another sack of gold. Everyone in Odessa wondered where the gold was coming from. Some noted that his shorter trips couldn't have taken him to the Guadalupe range and back, and that he must have buried a cache of gold closer to town. His longer trips were probably to the mine itself.

Sublett seems to have rediscovered a mine that had been known 200 years before, back when the Spanish had colonized the area. A certain Captain de Gavilan reported how an Indian had led him and 30 companions to a rich gold mine from which they took sacks full of gold. However, during the great Pueblo Revolt of 1680, rebellious Indians wiped out the Spanish settlements, and the secret of the gold mine died with the Spanish. By the time whites were settling the region, the Guadalupe range was a refuge for hostile Apache, and it was said that they knew the secret of the mine and jealously guarded it. Geronimo himself used to brag that his people had the biggest gold mine in the country, so it remains unclear how Sublett was able to return to the mine so many times without getting an arrow in his gut.

Geronimo

Whatever the case, riches didn't change Sublett at all. He never bought much for himself except booze, and his children were cared for but never spoiled. He seemed indifferent to the things riches could buy. What really interested him was the attention his mysterious gold brought him. He often said that he would never reveal the secret of his mine because he wanted people talking about him long after he died.

Of course, many people tried to get him to spill the beans. People would ply him with questions when he was drunk, and people would follow him out of town. A couple of times people even demanded the secret at the point of a gun. He evaded them all, usually by playing a drunken clown who couldn't speak coherently. More and more, that wasn't an act; old Ben Sublett did little with his fortune except drink it, and drinking was what eventually killed him.

Despite using the gold to care for his children, he never gave them more than they needed and only once did he take one of his kids to the mine itself. The honor went to his son Rolth Ross Sublett, who at the tender age of 9 was led through the forbidding mountains to see the secret to the Sublett family wealth. Rolth recalled, "The last stage to it, going west from the Pecos, was always made on horseback or with pack burros. It was down in a crevice, and the only way to get to it was by a rope ladder that my father always removed as soon as he came up with the gold. I played around while he got the ore out of a kind of cave. I seem to remember, too, that pieces of ore were in plain sight right in front of the cave. I am confident the mine is within six miles of a spring in the Rustler Hills."

That's a good clue for treasure hunters out there, as the Rustler Hills are 40 miles east of Guadalupe Peak. While many people have sought the gold around the peak itself since it's such a visible landmark, Rolth says the hidden mine lay to the east. Whether that spring he mentioned is still there after all these years is another question; springs come and go in the desert, and with the water table going down thanks to all the drilling and population expansion in Texas in the past century, there's a good chance it's gone. It must be noted that Rolth himself couldn't remember exactly where the mine was, and when he asked his father as he lay on his deathbed, old Ben waved him away and said he'd have to find it himself. Rolth tried several times before finally giving up.

Ben Sublett got a lot of criticism from the talkers around town for never letting his three children in on the secret of the mine, but his descendants defend his decision. They assert that the mine never brought him happiness, and he worried that it would have the same effect on his children. He wanted them to make their own way in the world and develop a proper work ethic. Sublett didn't want his legacy to be a trio of spoiled good-for-nothings.

While Sublett was an old rebel, he made his fortune from the earth, not from his fellow Confederates, but not all Confederates were so honest. As the Confederacy collapsed in 1865, rebel soldiers buried hordes of gold and silver, hoping to come back and retrieve them once things had settled down. Sometimes they buried guns along with the treasure for a planned revival of Southern independence, but typically, the only motivation was personal wealth.

Tales of Confederate treasure are especially persistent in the West, where many Confederate states were not occupied by Union forces until after peace was declared. The West also held out a bit longer; while General Robert E. Lee had his famous meeting with General Ulysses S. Grant at Appomattox Court House on April 9, 1865, it took some time for the other rebel armies to lay down their arms. The Confederate Trans-Mississippi Department, commanded by Lt. Gen. E. Kirby Smith, didn't surrender until May 26, and the last holdouts of Confederate Indians under Brig. Gen. Stand Watie didn't give up until June 23. This gave treasure hoarders plenty of time to dig their holes, and there have been stories, search parties, and dubious treasure maps ever since.

One of the more intriguing tales of Confederate gold, and one that's actually based on hard fact, is the story of the missing Texas state treasury. At the end of the war, Texas was in chaos as streams of hungry, ill-clothed rebel soldiers were heading home, and some turned to banditry. The roads were unsafe and there were riots in the cities. In the state capital of Austin, Governor Pendleton Murrah tried to convene the state legislature in order to repeal the ordinance of secession, but not enough representatives showed up. Fearing Yankee reprisals, he and other officials fled to Mexico. With no one in charge, Austin plunged into anarchy, and many of the state warehouses were looted.

Murrah

Confederate Captain George R. Freeman raised a small company of volunteers to restore order, and on June 11, he received a tip that the state treasury was going to be robbed. He summoned his men, numbering 20, and got to the treasury building just in time to catch about 50 robbers in the act of breaking open the safes. A gunfight ensued, Captain Freeman took a bullet in the arm, and one of the robbers was wounded. The rest of the outlaws escaped with about $17,000 in gold and silver, and they were last seen heading west towards Mount Bonnell.

Freeman

The thieves were never caught, but many believe that with Freeman's men hot on their trail, they had to bury the loot and scatter. Either way, the treasure was never recovered, and the question of whether the robbers ever managed to recover their money or if they fell prey to the dangerous times has been hotly debated ever since. Land developers on the outskirts of Austin should keep a close eye on what their bulldozers are uncovering.

It seems the legends of buried treasure will never die. As recently as the 1990s, an old rancher in New Mexico claimed to have discovered a hidden cave in the mountains. Which mountains? He wouldn't say. The interior of the cave was all covered with ice and felt like the inside of a meat locker. At the back of the cave lay several Aztec mummies, all perfectly preserved thanks to the low temperature. According to his story, these mummies must have been from the Aztec royal family because they were surrounded by a treasure that would put King Tut's to shame. The rancher's flashlight illuminated gleaming gemstones and sparkling silver necklaces, as well as heaps of gold chalices and plates.

Chapter 2: Bumbling Bandits and Freaky Fellers

The Wild West is famous for its outlaws. Jesse James, the Dalton gang, Billy the Kid, and dozens of others secured their place in history through their daring robberies and narrow escapes from the law, but for every Butch Cassidy and Sundance Kid, there were a dozen incompetent wannabes.

Two of the dumbest were Ernie and Oscar Woodson, a pair of teenaged brothers from Phoenix who were obviously reading dime novels instead of their schoolbooks. They decided to be Wild West outlaws and rob a train, but the problem was they made their attempt in 1910, not 1870, and Phoenix was no longer a frontier town. By then, Phoenix was a booming city with electricity, telephones, and the rule of law. The days of robbing trains were a thing of the past, and there hadn't been a train robbery in Arizona in years.

None of this dissuaded Ernie and Oscar. Too lazy to go find a major interstate train that might be carrying shipments of gold or a payroll, they simply boarded the commuter train that ran from Phoenix to Maricopa. They had left a pair of horses further down the line and they sat like well-behaved boys until the train approached the place where their getaway horses were hidden. Then they whipped out their pistols and with a jaunty air told the passengers to put their hands up.

The passengers obliged, and Ernie and Oscar got away with about $300. They even robbed the sheriff of Gila County, who was coming home from work at the time. Needless to say, the sheriff didn't take kindly to this, and as the brothers rode off in what they thought was a gallant style, the sheriff got off the train and made a few phone calls. The local sheriff, Carl Hayden of Maricopa County, quickly gathered up a posse, and some of the men rode after the brothers while Hayden grabbed a friend who owned an automobile and drove off in hot pursuit.

Sheriff Hayden

    The newfangled contraption came in handy, because as the Woodson brothers' horses and the posse's horses tired in the Arizona heat, Hayden and his friend sped through the mesquite and cacti without a problem and soon caught up with the boys, who meekly surrendered as soon as they saw the business end of Hayden's pistol. Hayden went on to become a senator, and he always bragged that he was the first man to foil a train robbery with an automobile.

    Hayden was also famous for making the Native Americans wear pants when they came into town. Most only wore a breechcloth, and that was upsetting the local ladies in an age when it was fashionable to cover up from neckline to ankle no matter what the temperature. Down in Tucson, they had problems with the Pima tribe showing too much leg as well, so they designated a "pants tree" just outside of town where they left some old pants for the tribe when they came in to trade. Making their legs sweat in the Arizona summer heat when it was perfectly logical to keep one's legs cool and bare was obviously one of the more trivial cruelties inflicted on the Native Americans by unsympathetic whites.

While the Woodson brothers have all but faded from memory, another bumbling bandit went on to lasting fame. His name was Elmer McCurdy, a man who accomplished more dead than alive. Born in 1880, this hard drinker from Maine wasn't amounting to much in life and drifted west in the hopes of a better future, but his drinking kept him from finding much work, so in 1907 he decided to enlist in the Army. While stationed at Fort Leavenworth, Kansas, he was trained in using a machine gun and also in demolitions, but after his stint in the Army, he again couldn't find work and thus decided to use his demolitions knowledge to blow up safes instead.

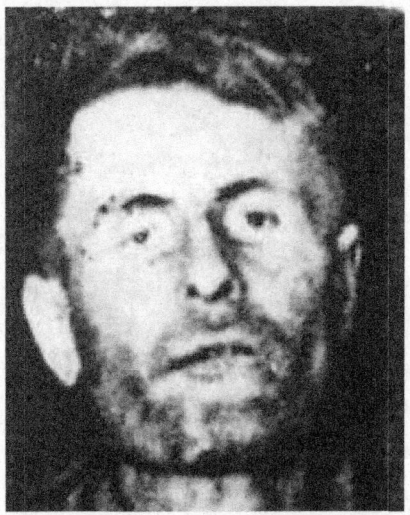

McCurdy

McCurdy must not have been a very good student in Explosions for Beginners, because when he and his gang stopped a train in Oklahoma in 1911 and tried to blow up its strongbox, McCurdy used too much nitroglycerine. There was a tremendous explosion, and burning bits of banknotes fluttered everywhere, but luckily for them there were about $450 worth of silver coins in the safe that was now melted into a gleaming blob of precious metal. They chipped this off the wall of the safe and made their escape.

McCurdy tried to rob another train later that year, and this time the train was supposed to be carrying nearly $400,000. It seems McCurdy and his two accomplices were so eager to strike it rich that they stopped the first train they saw and discovered it was the wrong train. Instead of carrying huge heaps of cash, it was only carrying a few passengers, and the bandits only got away with $46, a revolver, a coat, a watch, and two jugs of whiskey.

Disappointed, McCurdy hid out at a friend's farm, where he made quick work of two jugs of whiskey, but someone had recognized him on the train and soon there was a warrant out for his arrest and $2,000 on his head. Three sheriffs tracked him with bloodhounds to the hayloft where he lay in a drunken stupor. Knowing that he was armed and theoretically dangerous, they decided to wait for him to come out.

While McCurdy may have lacked intelligence and luck, he didn't lack a fight. When he finally realized he was surrounded, he opened fire on the lawmen and kept up a gunfight for an hour before taking a bullet in the chest. The sheriffs crept into the barn and found him dead, and a nearly empty jug of whiskey sat by his side, a loyal friend to the last. Sheriff Benton later recalled, ""It began just about 7 o'clock. We were standing around waiting for him to come out when the first shot was fired at me. It missed me and he then turned his attention to my brother, Stringer Fenton. He shot three times at Stringer and when my brother got under cover he turned his attention to Dick Wallace. He kept shooting at all of us for about an hour. We fired back every time we could. We do not know who killed him...(on the trail) we found one of the jugs of whiskey which was taken from the train. It was about empty. He was pretty drunk when he rode up to the ranch last night."

McCurdy's body was taken to a funeral home in Pawhuska and kept for a time as the funeral director preserved the corpse and waited for someone to claim it. No one did. In order to make up for his financial loss, the funeral director put a rifle in McCurdy's hands, stood him up, and charged admission to see him, even encouraging people to put nickels in the corpse's mouth. Not being the squeamish sort, the funeral director would pluck the coins out after the visitors went home. McCurdy now had a new life as "The Bandit Who Wouldn't Give Up."

This went on for almost five years until one winter's day in 1916 when two men showed up claiming to be McCurdy's brothers. They paid the outstanding fees and took McCurdy away for "a decent burial." In reality, they were James and Charles Patterson, owners of a traveling carnival in need of a new sideshow. McCurdy was exhibited throughout the country, sold to various other shows, and dressed up in all sorts of ways. In 1933, he was bought by film director Dwain Esper and stuck in theater lobbies as a "Dead Dope Fiend" to promote Esper's film *Narcotic!* The old boozehound had found new life warning America's youth of the dangers of drugs.

As McCurdy continued to change hands, he began to look a little worse for wear. His skin was shriveled and flaking, and the tips of his ears and some of his fingers and toes had blown off in a windstorm. McCurdy's various owners tried to fix him up by waxing him, painting him, and even adding fake digits, but he continued looking less and less lifelike. In fact, at some point people forgot he was a real corpse, and by 1976, he was no longer a bandit or a dope fiend but a dusty old prop hanging in the "Laff in the Dark" exhibition at The Pike amusement park in Long Beach, California. That year, a TV crew was filming an episode of *The Six Million Dollar Man* inside the attraction when one of the crew moved McCurdy. His arm fell off and the crewman was shocked to see real bone and muscle inside.

The police and coroner made a thorough investigation, and McCurdy may have become one of America's greatest mysteries if the coroner hadn't checked inside the mouth and found tickets to the 140 W. Pike Side Show and Louis Sonney's Museum of Crime. Louis Sonney was still alive and remembered that this painted, waxed, shriveled corpse had once been Elmer McCurdy, the prime attraction in the Museum of Crime.

McCurdy was finally laid to rest in 1977 at a solemn service with about 300 people in attendance. He now lies (hopefully forever) at the Boot Hill of Summit View Cemetery in Guthrie, Oklahoma, right next to Bill Doolin, a much more successful outlaw and founder of the Wild Bunch, at least until he was killed by a shotgun blast in a shootout with police. As fate would have it, every member of the Wild Bunch met a similarly violent death.

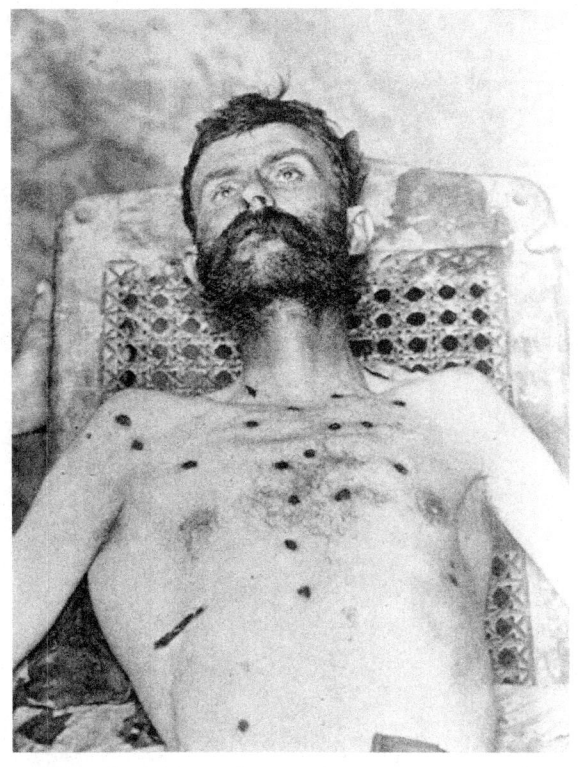

Doolin's corpse

Bleeding hearts like to say that people commit crimes as a way to get attention, a sort of cry for help in an uncaring world, but Leonard Borchardt tried to get attention in a different way and found the world sure was uncaring. This German Jewish immigrant moved to San Francisco and in 1884 took on the stage name Oofty Goofty, "the wild man from Borneo". He put on quite an act, covering his entire body with tar and horsehair and shouting out "Oofty Goofty!" while sitting in a cage and eating raw meat. According to a *Houston Daily Post* article from January 10, 1897, one member of the audience wasn't fooled by his act and cried out, "We can see a Jew for less than a quarter. What the devil are they givin' us?" The audience member then jabbed Oofty Goofty with his cane, and others followed suit until Oofty Goofty fell out of character and started cursing the audience in language unfit for any self-respecting wild man from Borneo.

Borchardt would have continued with the act but his costume got the better of him, as the tar he used to stick on the horsehair wouldn't allow him to sweat. When his body got overheated, doctors were called in to scrape and pull the tar off poor Oofty Goofty. Eventually they had to dunk him in solvent. After that, Borchardt decided to change his routine. In 1886 he tried to break the record for walking across the country pushing a wheelbarrow, but he was beaten up by a group of hayseeds on the second day of his trip. Undaunted, he went on to win several long-distance walking competitions, once walking 223 miles in six days.

When walking didn't pay enough, Borchardt hit on another idea. He claimed he couldn't feel any pain, and it's unclear whether this was true or not, but he sure could pretend he didn't. He'd go around saloons challenging anyone to make him cry out. It cost a nickel to kick him, 15 cents to hit him with a cane, and a whole quarter to bludgeon him with a baseball bat. In 1891 he met his match with heavyweight boxing champion John Sullivan, who hit him so hard with a billiard cue that he fractured three vertebrae and walked with a limp for the rest of his life. True to his word, he still didn't cry out in pain.

Sullivan

By all accounts Oofty Goofty was a law-abiding citizen who wanted to make it big in show business and failed, while Elmer McCurdy was a failed robber who inadvertently made it big in show business. However, the story of Joaquin Murieta and Three-Fingered Jack proved that someone can be both a successful outlaw and make it big in show business.

Joaquin Murieta was one of the baddest men ever to ride the West. Like many people, Murieta came to California from his native land of Mexico in 1850 in search of gold, but he was shocked when he learned later that a Foreign Miners Tax had been passed. It required foreigners to pay three dollars a month for the honor of breaking their backs in the mines. This was a lot of money back then, and many miners couldn't afford it. His white neighbors went one further and tried to convince him that the law meant it was illegal for Mexicans to stake a claim in the gold fields. Murieta decided to ignore the racist whites and kept digging before his neighbors showed up with guns and told him to head south.

Murieta was so enraged that he gathered a group of other dispossessed Mexican miners and started raiding the gold fields, killing white miners and stealing their gold. With his right-hand man Three-Fingered Jack, he led his desperados on an epic wave of crime that netted them more than $100,000 in gold, about a hundred horses, and left 19 men dead. The gang eluded pursuit for more than two years, getting into several scrapes with the law and killing three officers. Finally the governor created the California Rangers in 1853 to get rid of them.

The rangers caught up with them on July 25, 1853 near Panoche Pass in San Benito County, and there was a furious gunfight in which both Murieta and Three-Fingered Jack fell. The lawmen cut off Murieta's head and Jack's hand, put them in a jar full of brandy, and brought them back to town as proof that they'd killed the famous outlaws. Several locals recognized the head, and no one could dispute the hand, so the lawmen were able to collect a $5,000 reward, enough to buy sufficient brandy to pickle hundreds of heads.

The head and hand then made the rounds as a sideshow attraction. It cost $1 to see them, which wasn't cheap at the time, and they were finally purchased by the owner of the Golden Nugget Saloon in San Francisco, who put them behind the bar in order to attract customers. There's no record of whether that helped sales of brandy, but sadly, the head of Joaquin Murieta and the hand of Three-Fingered Jack were lost when the saloon was destroyed in the terrible earthquake of 1906.

An artist's depiction of Joaquin Murieta

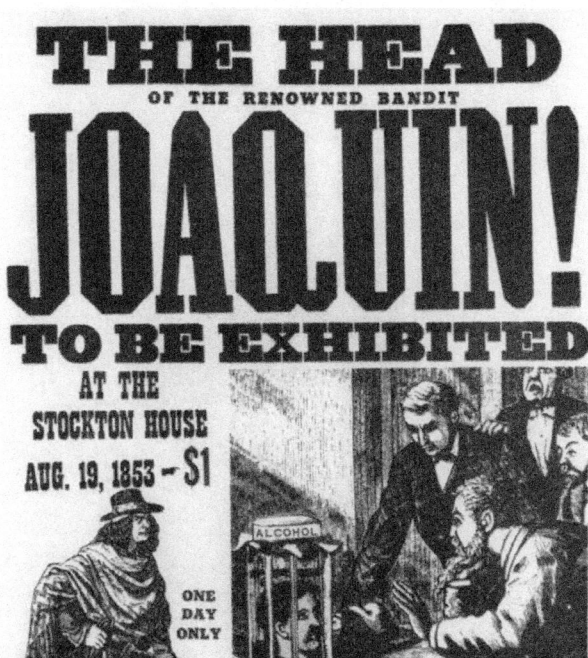

An advertisement at the time

Chapter 3: Jesse James is Alive

The Wild West has made legends out of many men after their deaths, but like Wild Bill Hickok, Jesse James was a celebrity during his life. However, while Hickok was (mostly) a lawman, Jesse James was and remains the most famous outlaw of the Wild West, with both his life of crime and his death remaining pop culture fixtures.

Like many icons of the Wild West, much of the legend of Jesse James is wrapped up in myth. He lived in an era when Americans on the East Coast clamored for tales of the West, whether the tales were true or not. However, unlike some western icons that were tagged as being outlaws far more dangerous than they really were, Jesse James was built up to be a more chivalrous bandit than he was in real life. The fact is that Jesse James was a cold-blooded killer who did not, contrary to legend, steal from the rich to give to the poor. He robbed the rich and poor alike, all for his own personal gain.

James and his notorious older brother Frank were Confederate bushwhackers in the lawless region of Missouri during the Civil War. Despite being a teenager, James was severely wounded twice during the war, including being shot in the chest, but that would hardly slow him down after the war ended. As he recuperated, some of the men he was known to associate with during the war robbed Clay County Savings Bank in Liberty, Missouri in 1866. While it's still unclear whether James was involved, he was soon conducting his own bank robberies.

Young Jesse became notorious in 1869 after robbing the Daviess County Savings Association in Gallatin, Missouri, during which he murdered the bank cashier in the mistaken belief that the cashier was Union officer Samuel Cox. Despite being officially branded an outlaw, public resentment with government corruption and the banks helped turn James into a celebrated "Robin Hood" type of robber, despite the fact he never actually gave anyone money.

Eventually James, his brother and their infamous gang became the most hunted outlaws in the country. In 1881, Jesse moved his family back to Missouri, settling in a small house in St. Joseph. He and Frank felt like the law was getting too close for comfort and it was time to leave Tennessee, but Frank did not join Jesse. He went on to Virginia. Now Jesse was without his brother, as well as the sympathy from citizens in his home state that had helped him elude the law the first time around. Many considered him to be a nuisance at best and dangerous at worst, and the new Missouri governor, Democrat Thomas T. Crittenden, persuaded railroad executives to pitch in on a $10,000 reward for Jesse and Frank. That money would prove to be tempting for someone who knew the famous outlaw.

By early 1882, Jesse was trying to put together yet another new gang, but he was running out of options. Now just a loose band of common thieves, Jesse was not even sure that he could trust the men in his gang. He grew increasingly paranoid and even murdered one of the members of his gang, Ed Miller. Convinced that Jim Cummins was out to get him, too, Jesse was in the process of hunting him down. The only two men that he thought he could really trust were Bob and Charley Ford. What Jesse did not know when he offered the Fords the chance to take part in robbing the Platte City Bank is that they had already agreed to a deal with Governor Crittenden.

Crittenden

Bob Ford was able to get a meeting with the governor through his sister Martha Bolton, who had been the object of a gun battle with Bob and a man named Dick Liddil, which resulted in the death of Wood Hite. With Bolton's assistance, Bob Ford negotiated a deal with Crittenden, who told him that if James was killed, the reward money that had been put up by the railroads would belong to him. Crittenden also mentioned that if Ford happened to be the one to ensure that Jesse was killed, he had the authority to pardon him. Bob convinced Charley that they should kill Jesse and get the reward money. Incredibly, the governor of Missouri had conspired to murder Jesse James.

Bob Ford

On the morning of April 3, 1882, Charley and Bob Ford were at Jesse's home in St. Joseph. Zee prepared breakfast for the men as Jesse got ready for a robbery that he had planned. Charley reportedly broke out into a sweat, causing Zee to comment and ask him if he was sick. Meanwhile, Jesse had taken off his gun belt to avoid drawing too much attention as he went in and out of his house. For Jesse to be without his guns was a rare occasion, but he gave the Ford brothers their opening. As Jesse climbed on to a chair to dust a picture, Bob and Charley drew their guns and approached him from behind. Bob shot Jesse point blank in the back of the head. Hearing the shot, Zee ran into the room and screamed, "You've killed him." Bob Ford's immediate response was "I swear to God I didn't." His curious remark aside, Jesse James was dead.

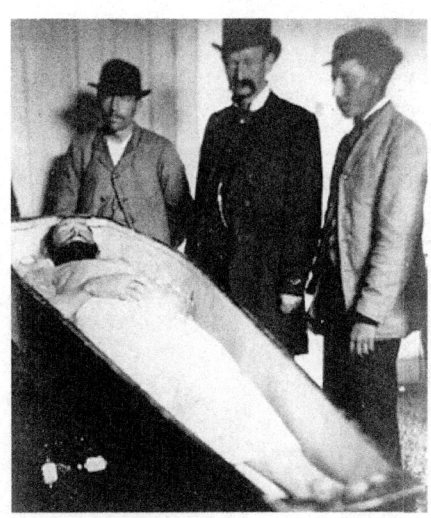

Jesse's body in a coffin

The Ford brothers surrendered to authorities and were convicted of murder, but Crittenden kept his word, and they were promptly pardoned and received some but not all of the $10,000 reward. However, the glory and notoriety they anticipated would come their way didn't materialize in the way they hoped. The Ford brothers initially billed themselves as the men who killed Jesse James and attempted to profit off of it by reenacting the murder and posing for photographs, but as was often the case in Jesse's lifetime, the public sided with him and was horrified at the cowardly way Bob Ford took Jesse's life. Bob was forced to leave Missouri in shame. Four years later, Charley Ford, done in by the stigma attached to what was called one of the most cowardly deeds in Missouri history, shot himself in the weeds near his home in Richmond, Missouri.

At the behest of Jesse's mother, the inscription on Jesse's tombstone read "Jesse W. James. Died April 3, 1882. Aged 34 years, 6 months, 28 days. Murdered by a traitor and a coward whose name is not worthy to appear here." Those who attended his funeral had no doubts, however, and friends, relatives, and old enemies came from all over to see Jesse in his casket. None of them ever questioned whether the man who lay before them was the same man who had terrified bankers and train managers for almost two decades.

Nonetheless, many people throughout the nation didn't believe Jesse was actually dead; after all, the outlaw's death had been reported several times before, only for Jesse to turn up again with a gun in one hand and stolen money in the other. Furthermore, despite all of the evidence suggesting he was dead, this was America, land of show business, and if someone could make an easy dollar making up a story that they were Jesse James, that was easier than robbing a train and possibly just as profitable. Several people went on the lecture circuit claiming they were Jesse and that they had dodged the fatal bullet. The most common story was that someone had been killed in his place so that Jesse could live a free life without fear of the law. Why Jesse would then go on tour telling everyone this was a question that was quietly avoided.

The most famous and brazen of these imposters was J. Frank Dalton, a carnival barker from Texas who knew a bit about show business. He had never been able to make a fortune, however, and he grew into an old man without any savings. In 1948, he came up with his most brazen and successful show by claiming to be Jesse James. Jesse would have to be about 100 years old at the time, but that didn't seem to bother the audiences as Dalton had studied the James legend and could spin all sorts of wild tales of his exploits, mixing fact in with the fiction to make it sound more plausible. He claimed that an outlaw named Charles Bigelow, who looked much like Jesse James, was the man Bob Ford had actually killed, and that Ford got the reward money while James was free of the law. Everyone came away happy, except Bigelow, of course. According to Dalton, after his faked death, Jesse laid low for a time and then continued his life of adventure by traveling the world and flying a fighter plane in World War I, even though he was already in his 60s.

Dalton

Dalton's gig was utterly ludicrous, but his song and dance made it big, and he landed interviews on national radio shows and gigs at state fairs. He returned to Missouri to act as a promoter for Meramec Cavern, the site of one of his supposed hideouts. The cave hosted a 102nd birthday party with the outlaw that was a media sensation, attended by a huge crowd as well as various other people claiming to be aged veterans of Jesse's band of robbers.

By 1950, the years were catching up with Dalton and he cut a sad figure, slumped in bed surrounded by old guns and photos. As a final bid for fame, he applied to a Missouri judge to have his name officially changed from J. Frank Dalton to Jesse James. The judge, R. A. Brauer of Franklin County, wasn't taken in like the gawpers at Meramec Cavern. Brauer ruled, "This court is called upon to change a man's name when there is nothing to change because he has never changed it, and by law it has never been changed from Jesse James to anything else. If he isn't what he professes to be, then he is trying to perpetrate a fraud upon this court. If he is Jesse James…then my suggestion would be that he retreat to his rendezvous and ask the good God above to forgive him so he may pass away in peace when his time comes."

J. Frank Dalton did pass away in peace in Texas in 1951. He claimed to be Jesse James until the very end, and his grave has that name written on it. While most historians scoff at the idea that he was Jesse James, nobody really knows who he was. The name J. Frank Dalton could very well have been an alias, another show business trick to make him sound like another famous outlaw of the same name. To this day, Dalton and his tall tale still have supporters.

As it turned out, it took very little time for Jesse's own family to cash in on his name. His mother was offered $10,000 by a promoter for her son's body, presumably to put the deceased outlaw on public display. Zerelda gave it some consideration, but opted instead to have Jesse buried in her front yard where she could watch over his grave. When sightseers and the curious came by to visit Jesse's final resting place, Zerelda sold them pebbles from the gravesite for a few cents each. When she ran out of pebbles, she replenished her supply from the alley behind her house.

Zee James was offered money to write a book about her husband, but despite needing the money, she refused to and would end up dying poor. Jesse's son wrote *Jesse James, My Father* in 1899. The first movie about Jesse appeared in 1908 when *The James Boys of Missouri* was released. The film was 18 minutes long, and taking into account that Jesse was still a sympathetic figure to many, the portrayal of him as an outlaw was done lightly. It was also a successful play for several years. This began a string of dozens of movie and television portrayals of Jesse or characters based on him that continued into the 21st century. Of all of the movies about him, Jesse's descendants claim that *The Assassination of Jesse James by the Coward Bob Ford*, starring Brad Pitt as Jesse in the last four months of his life, is the most accurate portrayal. The movie was adapted from a novel of the same name. Included in the film is the fact that Bob Ford went to New York to reenact the killing of Jesse James onstage, with his brother Charlie playing the role of Jesse.

In the wake of his notorious life and death, Jesse James was portrayed in several different was. Some viewed James as a symbol of resistance against government and industry, turning him into some sort of pre-Progressive Era rebel. Others viewed him as a symbol of the antebellum South whose life of crime was more about avenging the South and their lost way of life. It has taken time for some Americans to relinquish the image of Jesse James as a type of hero, which speaks to the deep wounds of the Civil War and the battle over the future of slavery as much as it does for Jesse's character. That Jesse lived and made his name as an outlaw during a time when there was such fascination with the West helped fuel his own need for attention and, in many respects, validation. Add into the mix the belief by those that sympathized with the Confederacy that he was a hero and the result is a legend.

However, that time has largely passed, and even as James remains perhaps the most famous outlaw of the West, glorified portrayals of him as heroic outlaw are now more about profiting off an interesting story than historical accuracy. New generations of Americans have come to view the antebellum South, the Civil War and the post-war bushwhacking much differently. In that context, Jesse James was hardly a hero, and despite his attempts to portray himself as such, he was not a victim. He was caught up in an era of change and did not like the change he saw.

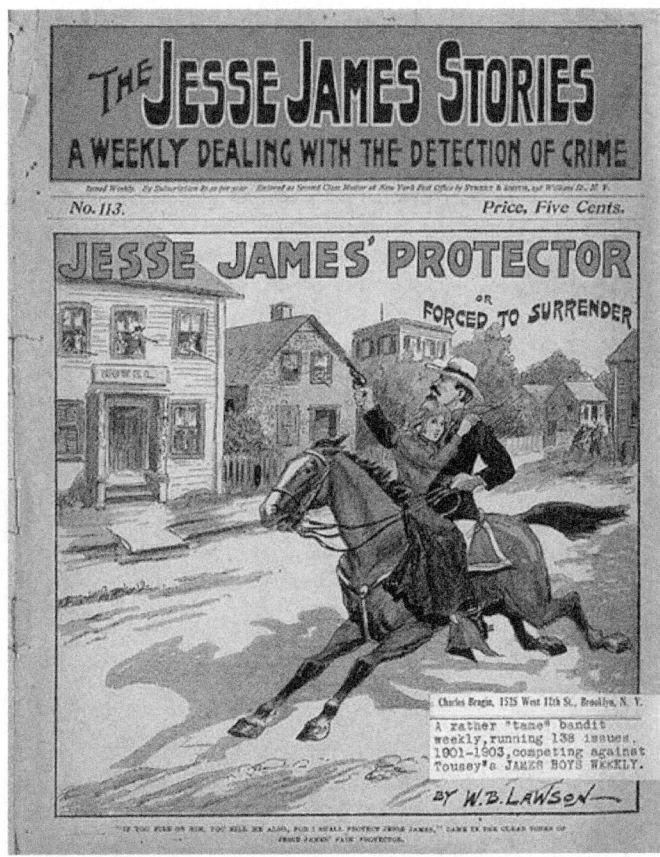

A 1901 dime novel about Jesse James

Chapter 4: So is Everyone Else

Jesse James wasn't the only Wild West outlaw to survive his own death; in fact, it seems like pretty much every Western bad man managed to live to a ripe old age.

In many ways, the narrative of the Wild West has endured more as legend than reality, and a perfect example of that can be found in the legend of William Henry McCarty Jr., better known as William H. Bonney or "Billy the Kid". Indeed, separating fact from fiction when it comes to the life of the West's most famous outlaw is nearly impossible, due in great measure to the fact that the young man himself cultivated the image of a deadly outlaw and legendary gunman himself. Though Billy the Kid may have killed anywhere from 4-9 men in his short life, he was often credited for killing more than 20.

With a wit as quick as his trigger, Billy the Kid had a bullet and a wisecrack for every man he killed, and his notoriety only grew when exaggerated accounts of his actions in Lincoln County eventually earned The Kid a bounty on his head. In December 1880, an ambitious buffalo hunter (and future Sheriff), Pat Garrett, helped track down and capture the famous outlaw, only for Billy the Kid to somehow escape jail shortly before his scheduled execution.

There was plenty of gunplay in the outlaw's life to help him become a well known if not celebrated figure in the West, but the legendary and controversial nature of his death has also helped him endure. A few months after his escape from jail, Billy the Kid was hunted down by Garrett in New Mexico once again, and it's still not completely clear whether The Kid was killed by Garrett in self-defense or simply murdered outright.

Billy the Kid

Billy became as famous for his ability to get out of a jam as he did for his marksmanship, escaping from custody no fewer than four times (once slipping out of handcuffs) and avoiding numerous ambushes. It seemed the law finally caught up with him at Fort Sumner, New Mexico on July 14, 1881, when lawman Pat Garrett tracked him down and put a bullet through his heart, or at least so he said. Numerous questions were raised about Garrett's story. It was pointed out that Garrett had grown embarrassed that he couldn't catch the outlaw and desperate for the reward money. Also, one of his deputies, John Poe, later said that he thought Garrett had shot the wrong man. Three inquests were held over the death, with many inconsistencies and even one witness later recanting his statement that the body he saw was that of Billy the Kid. Moreover, newspaper descriptions of the body did not match the known appearance of the outlaw.

Pat Garrett

Like with Jesse James, the gun smoke had barely cleared before people were announcing they were Billy the Kid and started selling tickets to crowds eager to hear their story. This continued for years, with even J. Frank Dalton getting in on the game before switching his story and claiming to be Jesse James. Most were obviously imposters out for a quick buck, but one man,

Ollie P. Roberts, popularly known as Brushy Bill Roberts, made many investigators sit up and take notice. The old timer living in Hico, Texas told his story to a lawyer in 1949, saying how Garrett had killed the wrong man and that he was the real Billy the Kid, and he did seem to know a lot about the outlaw's life. In 1950, Roberts met with New Mexico governor Thomas Mabry to ask for a pardon for his crimes, and in attendance were two sons of Pat Garrett. When the governor asked them if they wanted to question the supposed outlaw, one quipped, "I do not wish to dignify this claim with any questions." The governor then grilled Roberts, who struggled over several known facts about Billy the Kid.

Mabry ruled that Roberts was an imposter, and later investigators found census records showing he was much younger than Billy the Kid, having been born nearly two decades later in 1879. That should have been that, but there are researchers who to this day believe Roberts was actually Billy the Kid. They point out that Roberts had suffered a mild stroke before his questioning, which explains his confused answers. He could also do many of the things Billy the Kid could do, such as demonstrating his ability to escape from handcuffs and speaking Spanish fluently. Supporters also point to facial similarities between the two.

Another famous outlaw who some say escaped being killed by the law was Butch Cassidy. While the history books say he was gunned down along with the Sundance Kid in a shootout with the Bolivian army in 1908, many researchers doubt this story. The pair had led a gang of robbers in a string of bank and train robberies in the last two decades of the 19th century, but by 1901, Butch and Sundance had enough money and enough heat from the law that they decided to hightail it to Argentina, where they bought a ranch and settled down to honest living.

That honest living apparently didn't last long; by 1905 a pair of American outlaws were reported committing robberies. Historians suspect this was Butch and Sundance back to their old tricks, and that same year they sold their ranch and were on the run again. The Pinkerton Detective Agency had tracked them all the way to South America and was closing in. Butch and Sundance reemerged in Bolivia in 1908, robbing again, until they were cornered in a house by some Bolivian Army cavalry.

Butch Cassidy

The Sundance Kid

There was a shootout, with the cavalrymen pouring lead into the building until the return fire from inside slackened and died off. For a while there was silence except for agonized screaming coming from the house, suddenly cut short by a single shot. Another shot followed. After a time the Bolivians plucked up their courage, burst through the door, and found two white men riddled with bullets. The fatal shots had come from one of the bandit's own pistols. He had shot his companion in the head to put him out of his misery and then did the same to himself.

While everyone back in the United States assumed the two dead men were Butch and

Sundance, there is no direct evidence proving this. The Bolivians didn't have any pictures of them and thus had no way to identify them, and when an archaeologist tested the bones in the outlaws' graves, he couldn't find a DNA match to known descendents of Butch and Sundance.

Shortly after their supposed deaths, rumors began to spread that both men were alive and well. The rumors were especially strong about Butch Cassidy and came from no less a source than his own sister, who said he visited her several times after the 1908 shootout and died of natural causes in Washington state in the 1930s. Many people who knew him support these claims. Even Will Simpson, an attorney who prosecuted him in 1894, said he met with Cassidy long after the Bolivian gunfight. Some reports have him alive as late as 1945.

The South Americans beg to differ. Some say Butch was killed at his ranch in Argentina, while others say he was gunned down during a bank robbery in another part of the country. Folks in Paraguay say he retired to their country and died a peaceful death in 1935. The Chileans agree about the date, but say it was in their country. The Pinkertons didn't believe the Bolivians killed him either; they thought a man killed by police in Uruguay in 1911 was their guy.

Then came a further spin on the story. In 1934, a machinist in Spokane, Washington named William T. Phillips wrote a story titled *Bandit Invincible: The Story of Butch Cassidy* that told of how Cassidy survived the fight with the Bolivian cavalry (whom Phillips has catching them in the act of robbing a pack train, in contrast to what the Bolivian army report says) and that Sundance was shot dead. Cassidy got away and fled to Europe. Phillips even claimed to his son and neighbors that he was Cassidy himself, using the cover of fiction to reveal the truth about his exploits. While he didn't look much like Cassidy, the story goes that he fled to France and had plastic surgery. He then moved to Washington State and lived a quiet, law-abiding life until dying in 1937. He was cremated, so there's no chance of making a DNA match.

In 2011, a longer manuscript by Phillips came to light with many more details about Cassidy's adventures after his supposed death and pointed the finger more closely at Phillips and Cassidy being the same man. The rare book collector who discovered it noted many details of Cassidy's life that few, if anyone, knew but the bandit himself, and the manuscript made quite a splash with the press. Historians, however, weren't convinced, and Cassidy biographer Dan Buck told the Associated Press that the book is filled with historical errors and was "total horse pucky."

Chapter 5: Lost Civilizations

A strange article appeared in the usually sober *Arizona Gazette* in its April 5, 1909 edition, and it read as follows:

"EXPLORATIONS IN GRAND CANYON

Mysteries of Immense Rich Cavern being brought to light

Jordan is enthused

Remarkable finds indicate ancient people migrated from Orient

The latest news of the progress of the explorations of what is now regarded by scientists as not only the oldest archaeological discovery in the United States, but one of the most valuable in the world, which was mentioned some time ago in the Gazette, was brought to the city yesterday by G.E. Kinkaid, the explorer who found the great underground citadel of the Grand Canyon during a trip from Green River, Wyoming, down the Colorado, in a wooden boat, to Yuma, several months ago.

According to the story related to the Gazette by Mr. Kinkaid, the archaeologists of the Smithsonian Institute, which is financing the expeditions, have made discoveries which almost conclusively prove that the race which inhabited this mysterious cavern, hewn in solid rock by human hands, was of oriental origin, possibly from Egypt, tracing back to Ramses. If their theories are borne out by the translation of the tablets engraved with hieroglyphics, the mystery of the prehistoric peoples of North America, their ancient arts, who they were and whence they came, will be solved. Egypt and the Nile, and Arizona and the Colorado will be linked by a historical chain running back to ages which staggers the wildest fancy of the fictionist.

A Thorough Examination

Under the direction of Prof. S. A. Jordan, the Smithsonian Institute is now prosecuting the most thorough explorations, which will be continued until the last link in the chain is forged. Nearly a mile underground, about 1480 feet below the surface, the long main passage has been delved into, to find another mammoth chamber from which radiates scores of passageways, like the spokes of a wheel.

Several hundred rooms have been discovered, reached by passageways running from the main passage, one of them having been explored for 854 feet and another 634 feet. The recent finds include articles which have never been known as native to this country, and doubtless they had their origin in the orient. War weapons, copper instruments, sharp-edged and hard as steel, indicate the high state of civilization reached by these strange people. So interested have the scientists become that preparations are being made to equip the camp for extensive studies, and the force will be increased to thirty or forty persons.

Mr. Kinkaid's Report

Mr. Kinkaid was the first white child born in Idaho and has been an explorer and hunter all his life, thirty years having been in the service of the Smithsonian Institute. Even briefly recounted, his history sounds fabulous, almost grotesque.

'First, I would impress that the cavern is nearly inaccessible. The entrance is 1,486 feet down the sheer canyon wall. It is located on government land and no visitor will be allowed there under penalty of trespass. The scientists wish to work unmolested, without fear of archaeological discoveries being disturbed by curio or relic hunters. A trip there would be fruitless, and the visitor would be sent on his way. The story of how I found the cavern has been related, but in a paragraph: I was journeying down the Colorado River in a boat, alone, looking for mineral. Some forty-two miles up the river from the El Tovar Crystal canyon, I saw on the east wall, stains in the sedimentary formation about 2,000 feet above the river bed. There was no trail to this point, but I finally reached it with great difficulty. Above a shelf which hid it from view from the river, was the mouth of the cave. There are steps leading from this entrance some thirty yards to what was, at the time the cavern was inhabited, the level of the river. When I saw the chisel marks on the wall inside the entrance, I became interested, securing my gun and went in. During that trip I went back several hundred feet along the main passage till I came to the crypt in which I discovered the mummies. One of these I stood up and photographed by flashlight. I gathered a number of relics, which I carried down the Colorado to Yuma, from whence I shipped them to Washington with details of the discovery. Following this, the explorations were undertaken.'

The Passages

'The main passageway is about 12 feet wide, narrowing to nine feet toward the farther end. About 57 feet from the entrance, the first side-passages branch off to the right and left, along which, on both sides, are a number of rooms about the size of ordinary living rooms of today, though some are 30 by 40 feet square. These are entered by oval-shaped doors and are ventilated by round air spaces through the walls into the passages. The walls are about three feet six inches in thickness.

'The passages are chiseled or hewn as straight as could be laid out by an engineer. The ceilings of many of the rooms converge to a center. The side-passages near the entrance run at a sharp angle from the main hall, but toward the rear they gradually reach a right angle in direction.'

The Shrine

'Over a hundred feet from the entrance is the cross-hall, several hundred feet long, in which are found the idol, or image, of the people's god, sitting cross-legged, with a lotus flower or lily in each hand. The cast of the face is oriental, and the carving this cavern. The idol almost resembles Buddha, though the scientists are not certain as to what religious worship it represents. Taking into consideration everything found thus far, it is possible that this worship most resembles the ancient people of Tibet.

'Surrounding this idol are smaller images, some very beautiful in form; others crooked-necked and distorted shapes, symbolical, probably, of good and evil. There are two large cactus with protruding arms, one on each side of the dais on which the god squats. All this is carved out of hard rock resembling marble. In the opposite corner of this cross-hall were found tools of all descriptions, made of copper. These people undoubtedly knew the lost art of hardening this metal, which has been sought by chemicals for centuries without result. On a bench running around the workroom was some charcoal and other material probably used in the process. There is also slag and stuff similar to matte, showing that these ancients smelted ores, but so far no trace of where or how this was done has been discovered, nor the origin of the ore.

'Among the other finds are vases or urns and cups of copper and gold, made very artistic in design. The pottery work includes enameled ware and glazed vessels. Another passageway leads to granaries such as are found in the oriental temples. They contain seeds of various kinds. One very large storehouse has not yet been entered, as it is twelve feet high and can be reached only from above. Two copper hooks extend on the edge, which indicates that some sort of ladder was attached. These granaries are rounded, as the materials of which they are constructed, I think, is a very hard cement. A gray metal is also found in this cavern, which puzzles the scientists, for its identity has not been established. It resembles platinum. Strewn promiscuously over the floor everywhere are what people call 'cats eyes', a yellow stone of no great value. Each one is engraved with the head of the Malay type.'

The Hieroglyphics

'On all the urns, or walls over doorways, and tablets of stone which were found by the image are the mysterious hieroglyphics, the key to which the Smithsonian Institute hopes yet to discover. The engraving on the tables probably has something to do with the religion of the people. Similar hieroglyphics have been found in southern Arizona. Among the pictorial writings, only two animals are found. One is of prehistoric type.'

The Crypt

'The tomb or crypt in which the mummies were found is one of the largest of the chambers, the walls slanting back at an angle of about 35 degrees. On these are tiers of mummies, each one occupying a separate hewn shelf. At the head of each is a small bench, on which is found copper cups and pieces of broken swords. Some of the mummies are covered with clay, and all are wrapped in a bark fabric.

'The urns or cups on the lower tiers are crude, while as the higher shelves are reached, the urns are finer in design, showing a later stage of civilization. It is worthy of note that all the mummies examined so far have proved to be male, no children or females being buried here. This leads to the belief that this exterior section was the warriors' barracks.

'Among the discoveries no bones of animals have been found, no skins, no clothing, no bedding. Many of the rooms are bare but for water vessels. One room, about 40 by 700 feet, was probably the main dining hall, for cooking utensils are found here. What these people lived on is a problem, though it is presumed that they came south in the winter and farmed in the valleys, going back north in the summer.

'Upwards of 50,000 people could have lived in the caverns comfortably. One theory is that the present Indian tribes found in Arizona are descendants of the serfs or slaves of the people which inhabited the cave. Undoubtedly a good many thousands of years before the Christian era, a people lived here which reached a high stage of civilization. The chronology of human history is full of gaps. Professor Jordan is much enthused over the discoveries and believes that the find will prove of incalculable value in archaeological work.

'One thing I have not spoken of, may be of interest. There is one chamber of the passageway to which is not ventilated, and when we approached it a deadly, snaky smell struck us. Our light would not penetrate the gloom, and until stronger ones are available we will not know what the chamber contains. Some say snakes, but other boo-hoo this idea and think it may contain a deadly gas or chemicals used by the ancients. No sounds are heard, but it smells snaky just the same. The whole underground installation gives one of shaky nerves the creeps. The gloom is like a weight on one's shoulders, and our flashlights and candles only make the darkness blacker. Imagination can revel in conjectures and ungodly daydreams back through the ages that have elapsed till the mind reels dizzily in space.'"

While this article makes interesting reading, the Smithsonian has repeatedly denied that any such expedition took place. Of course, conspiracy theorists have accused the government of a cover-up, even if they are at pains to explain why a group of archaeologists would cover up the greatest archaeological find in American history. Most likely this newspaper story was made out of whole cloth, the type of tall tale many frontier hacks liked to spin for the enjoyment of their readers. How the usually staid and respectable *Arizona Gazette* got suckered by this is a matter for debate.

The Egyptians in the Grand Canyon aren't the only archaeological mystery of the West. Up in Wyoming, the native Shoshone tell of a tribe of little people less than 2 feet tall they called the Nimerigar. The Shoshone feared them because they'd come in swarms and fire poison-tipped arrows. They supposedly dwelled along the Wind River and San Pedro Mountains.

Many Native American tribes had their own legends of tiny, secretive tribes range from Ireland to Africa, but what makes the Nimerigar different is that one was discovered and examined by science. In 1934, two men were prospecting for gold in the San Pedro Mountains in the old Shoshone homeland. Using dynamite to blast through the rock, they uncovered a sealed cave 15 feet long, four feet wide, and four feet high. On top of a small ledge they saw a miniature mummy sitting with its legs crossed. It was only 6 ½ inches tall and probably would have stood 14 inches tall. It had a low, flat forehead, a flat nose, and a wide mouth with thin lips. The skin was brown and wrinkled, as is common for a human that has dried out through natural processes. Being left in a cave with a constant temperature and no exposure to the elements had kept it in a state of remarkable preservation. Even its fingernails were still attached. On top of its head there was a strange, dark, jelly-like substance. Photos show that it looks a lot like a little old man.

Dubbed the San Pedro Mountains Mummy, it became a hit on the sideshow circuit, where it was displayed under a glass bell jar. In 1950, the Pedro Mountains Mummy was lent to Dr. Harry Shapiro, curator of biological anthropology at the American Museum of Natural History. Shapiro gave it a scientific examination and X-rayed it. Dr. Shapiro sent the X-rays to Professor George Gill, a biological anthropologist at the University of Wyoming. Both scholars felt that the mummy was probably a newborn baby. This child probably died of anencephaly, a birth defect in which part or all of the brain is missing. Often part of the skull can be missing as well, so that jelly-like substance on the top of the head might have been exposed brain tissue. The researchers added that because of the head's deformity, making it more in proportion to the size of the body, it looked more like an adult than a baby.

Pictures of the mummy

That same year, the mummy was lent out to a private individual who claimed he wanted to study it. It was never returned and has since vanished. To this day, some people think the Pedro Mountains Mummy is proof that a race of tiny people once lived in the more remote regions of America.

Chapter 6: The Thunderbird

When white, black, and Hispanic settlers moved into North America, they often adopted tales from Native Americans into their own folklore. The Native Americans had been here first, after all, and while some dismissed their stories as "native superstition," others believed the original inhabitants of the land knew some of its secrets.

One of the more enduring stories is that of the Thunderbird, a giant supernatural bird with wings so large it makes a thunderous noise when it flies. There were many sightings of giant birds in the Old West over the years, and it appears the settlers meshed European tales of dragons with the Thunderbird legend.

The most famous Thunderbird story comes from this strange article that appeared in the *Tombstone Epitaph* on April 26, 1890:

"FOUND IN THE DESERT

"A STRANGE WINGED MONSTER DISCOVERED AND KILLED ON THE HUACHUCA DESERT

"A winged monster, resembling a huge alligator with an extremely elongated tail and an immense pair of wings, was found on the desert between the Whetsone and Huachuca mountains last Sunday by two ranchers who were returning home from the Huachucas. The creature was evidently greatly exhausted by a long flight and when discovered was able to fly but a short distance at a time. After the first shock of wild amazement had passed, the two men, who were on horseback and armed with Winchester rifles, regained sufficient courage to pursue the monster and after an exciting chase of several miles succeeded in getting near enough to open fire with their rifles and wounding it.

"The creature then turned on the men, but owing to its exhausted condition they were able to keep out of its way and after a few well directed shots the monster partly rolled over and remained motionless. The men cautiously approached, their horses snorting with terror, and found that the creature was dead. They then proceeded to make an examination and found that it measured about ninety-two feet in length and the greatest diameter was about fifty inches. The monster had only two feet, these being situated a short distance in front of where the wings were joined to the body.

"The head, as near as they could judge, was about eight feet long, the jaws being thickly set with strong, sharp teeth. Its eyes were as large as a dinner plate and protruded about half way from the head. They had some difficulty in measuring the wings as they were partly folded under the body, but finally got one straightened out sufficiently to get a measurement of seventy-eight feet, making the total length from tip to tip about 160 feet. The wings were composed of a thick and nearly transparent membrane and were devoid of feathers or hair, as was the entire body. The skin of the body was comparatively smooth and easily penetrated by a bullet.

"The men cut off a small portion of the tip of one wing and took it home with them. Late last night one of them arrived in this city for supplies and to make the necessary preparations to skin the creature, when the hide will be sent east for examination by the eminent scientists of the day. The finder returned early this morning accompanied by several prominent men who will endeavor to bring the strange creature to this city before it is mutilated."

No other article on this strange creature ever appeared in the *Epitaph*, even though it's safe to assume such a find would attract the interest of local scientists. By 1890, Arizona was shedding its frontier feel as more people settled there. A university had opened in Tucson, just 70 miles away and a quick journey by train, five years before. One would think the professors there would have rushed to examine the creature if they thought the article was real. It seems this story was in the nature of a joke, as any such find would have made it into the state and national press, not to mention scientific journals. Also, the ranchers would have been well aware that the preserved hide of the creature could sell for a high price.

That article doesn't mention any photographs, but several photos of supposed Thunderbirds have emerged over the years. Some show a giant bird tacked to the side of a barn, while others show what looks more like the pterodactyl familiar to paleontologists. There has been an outpouring of these on the Internet in recent years thanks to the ease of using photo software in adding images to existing old photographs. One shows a farmer holding up a little pterodactyl that looks like someone cut open an umbrella and glued a buzzard on the inside. Even photos known to be fake, such as one showing a group of Civil War soldiers proudly standing beside a pterodactyl they've shot down (created for the Fox TV show *Freaky Links*), have generated enthusiastic discussion on cryptozoology discussion forums.

The Tombstone incident wasn't the only Thunderbird sighting. The *Gridley Herald*, a California newspaper, reported in 1882 that two men named Joseph Howard and Thomas Campbell were cutting wood near Hurleton, California when they spotted something flying above the treetops. It looked like a crocodile, was 18 feet long with a 40-foot wingspan, and had six wings and 12 feet. Howard claimed he fired at it with his shotgun, and he told the newspaper, "It uttered a cry similar to that of a calf and bear combined, but gave no sign of being inconvenienced or injured. In fact, when the shot struck, we heard the bullets rattle as though striking against a thin piece of sheet iron." The editor opined, "This is the first time we have ever heard of such a creature as this, but our informants are reliable men, hence we cannot doubt their statements."

This wasn't the only flying monster supposedly hanging around California. There were persistent stories of a creature living in Lake Elizabeth, and rumors about this beast, which could both fly and live underwater, started with the Mexican settlers. The Lake Elizabeth monster was said to be as big as a whale, but with giant, bat-like wings, and the area was avoided because it was believed the creature would eat all the livestock.

Finally, in the 1880s, a brave man named Don Felipe Rivera tried to capture the creature in order to sell it for $25,000 to a circus. He found the monster by the lakeshore and fired at it with his Colt .44, but as with the other California monster, the bullets bounced off, making a ringing sound as if they were hitting metal. Don Felipe Rivera reported that he collected his bullets after the creature moved off, and that they were as flat as little pancakes. He said the creature had the head of a bulldog, six legs, and was about 45 feet long.

In 1891, there was a sighting of a pair of flying "dragons" in Fresno. They were 15 feet long and had rows of razor sharp teeth they used to bite chickens in half. There was a similar sighting in Utah in 1903.

Even today people still claim to see pterodactyls or other strange flying creatures in the West. There was a wave of pterodactyl sightings in Texas back in the 1970s, so if they didn't go extinct millions of years ago, maybe a few of the flying dinosaurs are still hiding out in the Lone Star State.

Chapter 7: Other Strange Creatures

The Thunderbird wasn't the only monster to appear in the Wild West. According to the lore, there was no shortage of strange creatures, some frightening, some bizarre, and some downright ridiculous.

In the ridiculous category is the fur-bearing trout, a tale that came from the mining camps of Colorado. There was one camp where an unusually high number of the miners were bald. Whether the miners were old or simply unlucky the story doesn't say. A hair tonic salesman headed to the camp one day in order to "mine the miners", as the old saying goes. During a gold rush (or even a lead rush), mining the miners was the best way to strike it rich, as mining camps sprung out of nothing and everything was in short supply. Anyone with a wagonload of canned goods, tools, and liquor could make money with more certainty than even the most diligent digger, so this hair tonic salesman figured this shiny-scalped mining camp would be his Mother Lode. He turned out to be smarter than he was lucky, however, because as he was crossing the Arkansas River he accidentally dropped his product in the water. The bottles broke and his hair tonic filled the river. Soon local fishermen discovered that the trout had grown hair, so instead of setting out a hook and bait, they set up barber poles by the side of the river. The fur-bearing trout, desperate to get rid of their hair and go back to their natural scaly baldness, leapt out of the water and the fishermen collected them.

Some say the bald miners wanted to get a bit of that hair tonic and rubbed the fur-bearing trout on their hairless pates in the hopes of a cure. One penniless miner named Shoeless Magee, whose feet were as bare as his head, accidentally dropped a fish on his feet and ended up with hair on his feet as well as his head. He later hit the Mother Lode and retired in San Francisco. He attributed his change of fortune to the new hair the fur-bearing trout gave him and for the rest of his days could be seen walking the streets of San Francisco barefoot.

Then there's the Jackalope. This critter has the body of a jackrabbit and the antlers of a pronghorn antelope, hence the name. Most are the size of normal jackrabbits, but back in the old days some grew so big that cowboys could put bridles on them and hop around the prairie. There are postcard photos supposedly proving it, and postcard photos could never lie. Of course, catching and taming the average Jackalope is no easy task. Jackalopes are timid creatures and fool their pursuers by imitating human speech, saying things like "He's run behind that tree over yonder!" when in fact the critter had run behind a rock in the opposite direction. Some say the best way to lure him out is with whiskey.

Naysayers and curmudgeons claim that the Jackalope was actually invented by a hunter and amateur taxidermist named Douglas Herrick (1920–2003) from Douglas, Wyoming, who in 1932 killed a jackrabbit and decided to preserve it with an extra touch: a pair of antelope horns. He sold it to a local hotel and soon his Jackalopes were a big hit. In time, the Herrick family was selling Jackalopes by the thousand, and even the town of Douglas got in on the game by selling Jackalope hunting licenses.

The Ozarks in northern Arkansas and southern Missouri have long been a hideout for outlaws, Confederate guerrillas, and strange legends. The thinly populated region has thick underbrush, rough hills, deep valleys, and large swamps, so it's hardly surprising that locals tell many a strange story about what lurks in those hills. One of the strangest is about the Boggy Creek Monster. This is the local Bigfoot, a seven-foot-tall hairy beast with a strong, musky odor. It's found near the vicinity of the town of Fouke and has often been sighted around the creek that gives the monster its name.

Tales of the Boggy Creek Monster go back to the 1840s, and it was known for killing livestock and dogs, most likely for food. It was generally feared and many locals avoided the creek. Sightings continued for a century, so perhaps there's a whole family of Boggy Creek Monsters down there. A farmer who saw it in 1973 said it was only four feet tall, but most sightings say it's man-sized or larger, so this may have been a child. One woman who saw it in 1971 said it had long, dark hair and walked hunched over, swinging its arms like a monkey.

There was a wave of sightings in 1996, but those have died down in recent years. Sadly no photos exist, so any true believer has to be content with a 1972 film called *The Legend of Boggy Creek*. The film made a surprising amount of money and two more Boggy Creek movies were made.

While the Boggy Creek Monster never attacked humans, one of Arkansas' other legendary beasts is not so friendly. According to legend, strange being lurks beneath the muddy waters of the White River near the Ozarks town of Newport, 84 miles northeast of Little Rock. Known as the White River Monster, locals affectionately refer to it as Whitey. Most sightings describe it a giant serpent about 30 feet long with spines along its back. Three fishermen who saw it in 1966 said it had the head of a monkey and arm-like flippers, and many have remarked on the strange sounds it makes, described as a bellowing or a combination of a cow's moo and the neigh of a horse. The monster was known to the Quapaw Indians and once overturned one of their canoes. During the Civil War, when Arkansas was part of the Confederacy, Whitey proved himself to be a Yankee by overturning a Confederate gunboat.

Modern sightings, documented by local newspapers, began in 1915, and there have been sightings on and off ever since. There were about a hundred sightings in 1937, and one man who claimed he saw it was Bramlett Bateman, who owned a plantation by the river. He even opened up a viewing area, charging people a quarter to sit and stare out at the river. Being the hospitable sort, Bateman kept them refreshed with food and drinks, for a price of course.

In the early 1970s there was another wave of sightings and the first photograph of Whitey, a blurry image showing what looks like an alligator with oversized eyes swimming along the river. In 1971, some three-toed tracks measuring fourteen inches long were found along the muddy riverbank along with a lot of crushed underbrush as if a large animal had walked through it. Even some small trees had been broken, so the critter must have been pretty strong.

In 1973, the Arkansas State Legislature created the White River Monster Refuge to protect the creature. It lies next to Jacksonport State Park. People can't "molest, kill, trample, or harm the White River Monster while he is in the retreat."

America may not be the home of Loch Ness, but there are supposedly all sorts of lake monsters. It seems there isn't a lake, pond, reservoir, or oversized puddle that doesn't have its own monster skulking about in it. Cowboys used to say that if someone left an open barrel out in the rain before breakfast, there would be a lake monster in it by suppertime.

One of the more famous American lake monsters is the Bear Lake Monster in Utah, and stories of this 90-foot brown snake go back almost 200 years. It has a skinny head that's almost entirely one huge mouth, capable of swallowing a man in a single gulp. It's been known to eat swimmers but sometimes, if it's feeling playful, it will sneak up and blow a spout of water at them. It also has little legs along its sinuous body that it can use to scuttle along the land. One story claimed that a brave hunter tried to shoot it with his rifle but missed with every shot, as if the creature was magically deflecting the bullets. The hunter then did the smart thing by dropping his gun and hightailing it to the next county. The Bear Lake Monster ate his rifle and sunk back down beneath the surface. It hasn't been seen for many years, so perhaps it died of indigestion.

An even stranger lake monster is the Alkali Lake Monster. Alkali Lake, now known as Walgren Lake, is found in a volcanic region of Nebraska. The lake is only 50 acres in size and is popular among fishermen for its bullhead and largemouth bass, but it's a stranger fish that has earned notoriety. The Native Americans were well aware of something unusual in the lake, something that looked like a 40-foot gator with a gray skin and a big horn on its snout. Not even the bravest brave would paddle out into the lake's waters for fear of that terrible horn ripping through the bottom of his canoe. It would be lunchtime then, and not for the native.

Like many of America's lake monsters, this one has survived into the modern era. A sighting reported in the *Omaha World Herald* on July 24, 1923, by a Mr. J.A. Johnson said that he and two companions spotted the monster swimming through the lake. It must have spotted them too, because it let out an ear-splitting roar and disappeared beneath the surface. Johnson stated the creature was well known to the people of the area: "I could name forty other people who have also seen the brute."

In the desert Southwest, the Mexican community has passed down tales about the Chupacabra, which translates to "goat sucker". This small humanoid creature has been part of Mexican culture for centuries and may be based on Native American beliefs. The earliest report comes from 1540 and describes them as small men with dark scales. Each carried a torch and a spear and they would assemble in large numbers to attack settlements. Since then, the Chupacabra has been described in many ways according to the fashion of the time. In modern times he looks like a gray alien with fins on the back of its head and spine. As their name suggests, they suck the blood out of goats and other livestock.

Chupacabras became trendy in the 1990s, with sightings all over Latin America, especially Mexico, as well as the Southwest. In fact, Chupacabras seemed to follow the Mexican community wherever they went, and there were Chupacabra sightings in Mexican neighborhoods as far north as the Great Lakes region. Chupacabra t-shirts became all the rage and there was even a Chupacabra dance in Mexico.

Bibliography

Anderson, Dan. *One Hundred Oklahoma Outlaws, Gangsters, and Lawmen, 1839-1939.*

Gretna, LA: Pelican Publishing, 2014.

Charles River Editors. *The History and Folklore of Vampires: The Stories and Legends Behind the Mythical Beings*. 2014.

Chorvinsky, Mark. "Cowboys and Dragons: Unraveling the Mystery of the Thunderbird Photograph" in *Strange Magazine*, No. 21 (2000).

Cox, Patrick. "Treasury Robbery", *Handbook of Texas Online* (http://www.tshaonline.org/handbook/online/articles/jct03), accessed January 13, 2015. Uploaded on June 15, 2010. Published by the Texas State Historical Association.

Dobie, J. Frank. *Coronado's Children: Tales of Lost Mines and Buried Treasures of the Southwest*. Austin, TX: University of Texas Press, 1979.

Heatwole, Thelma. *Ghost Towns and Historical Haunts in Arizona*. Phoenix, AZ: Golden West Publishers, 1981.

Jameson, W.C. *Unsolved Mysteries of the Old West*. Lanham, MD: Taylor Trade Publishing, second edition, 2013.

Jameson, W.C. *Legend and Lore of the Guadalupe Mountains*. Albuquerque, NM: University of New Mexico Press, 2007.

Martin, Douglas. "Douglas Herrick, 82, Dies; Father of West's Jackalope" in *New York Times*, January 19, 2003.

McGaw, William C. *Southwest Saga: The Way it Really Was*. Phoenix, AZ: Golden West Publishers, 1988.

McLachlan, Sean. *It Happened in Missouri*. Second edition. Guilford, CT: Globe Pequot Press, 2013.

McLachlan, Sean. *Outlaw Tales of Missouri*. Second edition. Guilford, CT: Globe Pequot Press, 2014.

Morrow, Lynn, and Dan Saults. "The Yocum Silver Dollar: Sorting out the Strands of an Ozark Frontier Legend" in *Gateway Heritage* 5 (Winter 1984-1985).

Morrow, Lynn. "The Yocum Silver Dollar: Images, Realities, and Traditions." In *The German-American Experience in Missouri*, 159–76. Edited by Howard Marshall and James Goodrich. Columbia: Missouri Cultural Heritage Center No. 2, University of Missouri, 1986.

National Park Service press release, January 14, 2015. "Winchester Model 1873 Rifle

Recovered in Great Basin National Park." http://www.nps.gov/grba/parknews/upload/Jan-15-Rifle-Discovery-PR.pdf Accessed January 18, 2015.

Radford, Benjamin and Joe Nickell. *Lake Monster Mysteries: Investigating the World's Most Elusive Creatures.* Lexington, KY: University Press of Kentucky, 2006.

Schlosser, S. *Spooky Southwest: Tales Of Hauntings, Strange Happenings, And Other Local Lore.* Guilford, CT: Globe Pequot Press, 2004.

Silverberg, Robert. *Ghost Towns of the American West.* Athens, OH: Ohio University Press, 1994.

Steele, Philip W., and George Warfel. *The Many Faces of Jesse James.* Gretna, LA: Pelican Publishing Company, 1995.

Utley, Robert M. *Billy the Kid: A Short and Violent Life.* Lincoln, NE: University of Nebraska Press, 1989.

Wood, Joe. *My Jesse James Story.* Washington, MO: The Missourian Publishing Company, Inc., 1989.

Yeatman, Ted P. *Frank and Jesse James: The Story Behind the Legend.* Nashville, TN.: Cumberland House, 2000.

Printed in Great Britain
by Amazon